ARCHITECT

By Jessica Cohn

Content Adviser: Andy Tinucci, LEED
(Leadership in Energy and Environmental Design) Accredited Professional

Gareth Stevens
Publishing

Please visit our web site at **www.garethstevens.com**.
For a free catalog describing Gareth Stevens Publishing's list of high-quality books, call 1-800-542-2595 (USA) or 1-800-387-3178 (Canada).
Gareth Stevens Publishing's fax: 1-877-542-2596

Library of Congress Cataloging-in-Publication Data
Cohn, Jessica.
    Architect / by Jessica Cohn.
        p. cm. — (Cool careers: cutting edge)
    Includes bibliographical references and index.
        ISBN-10: 1-4339-1954-0   ISBN-13: 978-1-4339-1954-1 (lib. bdg.)
        ISBN-10: 1-4339-2153-7   ISBN-13: 978-1-4339-2153-7 (softcover)
        1. Architects—Juvenile literature. 2. Architecture—Vocational guidance—
    Juvenile literature. I. Title.
    NA2555.C54 2009
    720.23—dc22   2008052597

This edition first published in 2010 by
Gareth Stevens Publishing
A Weekly Reader® Company
1 Reader's Digest Rd.
Pleasantville, NY 10570-7000 USA

Copyright © 2010 by Gareth Stevens, Inc.

Executive Managing Editor: Lisa M. Herrington
Senior Editor: Brian Fitzgerald
Senior Designer: Keith Plechaty
Produced by Editorial Directions, Inc.
Art Direction and Page Production: Paula Jo Smith Design

Picture credits: Cover, title page, Andy Tinucci; p. 5 © Linda Matlow/Alamy; p. 8 © Robert Read/Alamy; p. 9 © Jupiterimages/BananaStock/Alamy; p. 11 © Neil Rabinowitz/Corbis; p. 12 John Lund/Marc Romanelli/Blend Images; p. 13 Andrew Lindy; p. 15 Chuck Choi/Arcaid/Alamy; p. 16 Glow Images/Alamy; p. 17 © Enigma/Alamy; p. 19 © Ellen McKnight/Alamy; p. 21 © H. Mark Weidman Photography/Alamy; p. 22 Chris Howes/Wild Places Photography/Alamy; p. 23 © 2008 J. B. Spector/Museum of Science + Industry; p. 24 © Douglas Kirkland/Corbis; p. 25 © David Zanzinger/Alamy; p. 26 iStock; p. 27 Mario Tama/Getty Images; p. 28 © Gondwana Photo Art/Alamy

Special thanks to architects Andy Tinucci and Rea Koukiou for the cover image. The photograph shows Koukiou, a intern who graduated from the University of Texas at Austin with a master's degree in architecture. It was taken by Tinucci of David Woodhouse Architects LLC, 230 W. Superior, 6th Floor, Chicago, IL 60654. Their web site is www.davidwoodhouse.com.

Printed in the United States of America

1 2 3 4 5 6 7 8 9 14 13 12 11 10 09

CONTENTS

Words in the glossary appear in **bold** type the first time they are used in the text.

CHAPTER 1

BIG PICTURE

Millennium Park in Chicago, Illinois, runs along the shore of Lake Michigan. The park is filled with outdoor stages and huge pieces of art. One piece of art looks like a giant fun-house mirror. The park's planners wanted people to notice and appreciate their surroundings. Outdoors or indoors, architects work to make space feel special.

What Architects Do

Architects work on many types of projects. Whatever the project, their job is to answer these questions: What is the purpose of the building or space? How can the design help improve the use of the building? What materials should be used? What is the setting? How will the weather affect the design? How much money will the project cost?

An architect's best projects add beauty to the world. They improve people's everyday lives. An architect must also handle many smaller details.

Architects carefully designed Chicago's Millennium Park. Find the piece of art that looks like a fun-house mirror.

"Architecture is a creative services business," says New York architect Dennis Wedlick. "That means that architects don't make things. They design things as part of a service that they provide their **clients**." Then they help their clients turn that design into a real building.

A Career Plan

People who want to be architects must earn a special degree. They also need a **license** to work as architects. At school, they learn to design structures and **sites**. An architect's goal is to make space work. The space should be easy and safe to use as well as beautiful.

Architects design outdoor spaces, such as Millennium Park in Chicago. They also work on indoor spaces, such as shopping malls. They plan big

An architect shows his client the building site.

structures, such as skyscrapers and sports stadiums. An architect might design a group of structures, such as a neighborhood of houses. Architects work on bridges, tunnels, and ships, too.

Where They Work

Architects often work in an office. There they meet with clients, coworkers, and experts in other fields. When the project gets under way, the architect will go to the site to oversee construction. **Landscape architects** often work outside to oversee their design of outdoor spaces.

On the Cutting Edge: Green Architecture

Today's architects have many things to consider. These days, you hear a lot about global warming. That is a worldwide rise in temperature. People believe pollution contributes to global warming. New construction has to last without hurting the planet.

To help the environment, more architects are using **renewable resources**. Renewable resources are materials and energy that replace themselves. Fast-growing grass called bamboo and sunlight are examples of renewable resources. Today, architects try to avoid using materials that are in limited supply. Buildings that use less energy are important to everyone.

The best buildings are built to last without wasting resources. Architecture that makes the most of Earth's resources is often called **green architecture**. Green buildings are designed to have less impact on people's health and the environment.

Is This Career Right for Me?

If you are thinking about becoming an architect, ask yourself these questions:

- Do you enjoy building things?
- Do you value art and the ways things look?
- Do you communicate your ideas well and work easily with others?
- Are you good at solving problems?
- Do you pay attention to little things?
- Do you have good judgment?
- Do you like organizing things?

A building worker uses stored rainwater to water the lawn. That's green architecture at work!

Planning Stages

Architects often stay involved in all steps of a project. Here are just a few of their tasks:

- Meet with a client to decide goals.
- Carry out studies about how the project will affect the environment.
- Prepare drawings and models.
- Come up with a **budget**.
- Present the plans to the client.
- Develop construction plans that follow building rules and laws.
- Rework plans as needed.
- Help the client hire builders and settle on costs.
- Work with the construction team on-site.

CHAPTER 2

TAKING ON THE CHALLENGE

I n Kirkland, Washington, a team of architects was designing a **condominium**. The project included shops and restaurants. The land was next to Lake Washington, so the architects needed to design a dock for boats as well. It was a big job.

There was another challenge. Common building materials made one of the condominium owners ill. The client got headaches around certain chemicals.

The architects went into action. To cut down on chemicals, they built with a lot of unfinished wood. They used special paint and glues. They brought in concrete blocks and natural stone. They set up special air-conditioning that cleaned the air. This project, completed in 1990, was an unusual case. For an architect, though, every job is a special challenge.

Form and Function

Architects first consider a structure's main purpose, or function. It might be to provide a place to live, work, or learn. Its function might be to offer a place to pray, listen to a concert, see art, or exercise. Or the structure

Architects built this unusual condominium on Lake Washington. They used unfinished wood and natural stone.

might have a completely different function, such as honoring war heroes with a monument.

Architects then consider other things, such as the budget. They listen to their clients' wishes. Finally, they create a design that satisfies the most needs. Architects must use their knowledge, imagination, and resources.

Ideas for Life

Good architects have many skills. They are creative and visual. They are also careful listeners who must consider many different needs. Architects have to work as part of a team as well as on their own.

Being able to draw is a plus. Drawings help architects communicate their ideas. Today's architect does much of that work using computer programs.

Architects think of creative answers to many different problems.

On the Job: Architect Dennis Wedlick

Dennis Wedlick started his own company in New York City in 1992.

Q: What kind of work do you do?

Wedlick: I design furniture, buildings, and public places. [But] much of my career has been spent helping people build their dream home.

Q: What do you like most about your career?

Wedlick: Helping people accomplish their dreams.

Q: What is difficult about the job?

Wedlick: The houses that we create are one-of-a-kind. ... You can't send a house back the way that you can return a sweater if it is not perfect. Our houses are more like a sweater a grandmother might make for a newborn granddaughter.

Q: What is special about your career?

Wedlick: It is a creative profession and a service profession at the same time. For example, I do more than just design houses for people. I help them find the perfect piece of land to buy. [I help them] decide what size house they need and figure out what they can afford. I find the best builder with the best prices. I oversee the house being built and then check to see that the house is holding up.

Q: What advice do you have for students who are thinking about this job?

Wedlick: [It is important] that you are a hard worker and that you like to work with people. You must have a thorough understanding of the principles of architecture. And you must have a sincere [love for] the benefits that good architecture brings to this world.

CHAPTER 3

STORIES THAT RISE

Every building has a story. The Hearst Building in New York City was six floors tall when it was built in 1928. The builders had planned for the first floors to be the base of a skyscraper. Then the Great Depression took place. Banks and businesses failed all over the world. There was not enough money to finish the project.

In 2006, the building's story took a happy turn. Construction teams added 40 floors, making the Hearst Building a skyscraper at last. The design for the new addition is different from the original plan. These days, people worry about pollution. They want buildings that do less harm to the environment. The new design made the new Hearst Building one of the city's first "green buildings."

Teamwork in Action

The bottom section of the Hearst Building is a historic structure. Before construction on the new addition began, architects carefully studied the original plans. Those plans were nearly 100 years old!

In the new design, architects made several changes. They added tubes under the floors. Water in those tubes heats the building in winter and cools it in summer.

Architects brought old and new together in New York City's Hearst Building.

Working as part of a team is what architects do.

The architects also used 10,480 tons of recycled steel. They worked closely with the steelmakers. They needed the frame to be strong but light.

Architecture is all about teamwork. The architects worked closely with their **engineers**. The team created a special steel frame. They made their frame from huge triangles of steel. The frame is strong but uses less steel than other designs.

Outside Elements

Special tanks collect and store rainwater from the roof of the Hearst Building. The rainwater is used

Digging In

Architecture school is not easy. Students at Yale University (below) have called their studies "archi-torture." That's because the professors have such high standards and the students have to work such long hours!

Architecture can be fun, too. At Australia's Curtin University, students tried to break the world record for the tallest tower made of sugar cubes. At Yale, a recent competition was to design a rest stop for travelers on the road.

to water the building's plants and the nearby trees outside the building.

The planners also thought about traffic flow outside the building. They improved a nearby subway station as part of their plan. They added elevators and fixed stairs.

The Hearst Building team won a gold LEED rating awarded by the United States Green Building Council (USGBC). LEED stands for Leadership in Energy and Environmental Design. The USGBC supports green architecture.

How to Become an Architect

If you are interested in working on a project like the new Hearst Building, you must first study at an architecture school. The National Architectural Accrediting Board (NAAB) has a list of all schools that meet their standards.

In architecture school, you will learn drawing, modeling, and graphic communication skills. You will also learn important computer programs. You will study art history and structural systems. You will learn the science of building and materials.

Building a Future

If becoming an architect interests you, study the job. Look for part-time work with architects

Landscape Architect

Fletcher Steele (1885–1971) was a famous landscape architect. He thought of gardens as outdoor living spaces. He believed that planning greenery was like music or art. He wrote that he wanted all his places "to be comfortable and if possible slightly mysterious by day ... appealing to the painter. I want them to be [wonderful] in the moonlight."

or engineers. Town building departments sometimes offer **internships**.

You will need a solid art, math, and science background. Take drafting, drawing, or art classes in high school. Try to find related summer camps. Build a file of your own artwork. Talk with architects. Learn about specialties, such as landscape architecture, that might interest you.

CHAPTER 4

SPECIAL SPACES

Frank Lloyd Wright (1867–1959) is one of the world's most famous architects. His designs work with nature. His buildings look as if they have grown up from the land. In his designs for more than 1,000 projects, Wright showed that "form and function are one."

Wright was famous for using new kinds of materials. He built with glass bricks and special concrete blocks. If you bought a Wright house, you bought his vision. He built homes in the hills and forests of the Midwest. He also designed large public structures, such as the unusual Guggenheim Museum in New York City.

Today, architects build on the ideas of architects like Frank Lloyd Wright. They test new materials. They make their own history.

Low-Impact Design

In school, you are taught to reduce, reuse, and recycle. Christopher Stafford is an architect who practices these rules. He has experimented with using mud, clay, and straw to build. He carefully considered the environment while building his own home in Washington state.

Architect Frank Lloyd Wright valued the role of nature in his work. He built this Fallingwater home partly over a waterfall!

Every choice matters for architects working on a building project. Making cement powder, for example, produces carbon dioxide, a colorless gas with no smell. Adding carbon dioxide to the air seems to add to global warming.

When Stafford needed to mix concrete for his basement, he replaced half of the cement powder with fly ash. Fly ash is a waste product from factories that burn coal. It worked! Stafford found a way to use trash that otherwise would have polluted the air and land.

Factories that burn coal produce a waste called fly ash. Some architects build with concrete that has fly ash in it.

A Smart Home

"Everyone should be able to have a green house," says architect Michelle Kaufmann. Her houses use renewable materials such as bamboo for the floor. They create a healthy environment for the people who live in them, too. Her houses are also **modular**. They are built in parts that get put together at the building site. Her designs win awards. One of her houses (above) is at the Chicago Museum of Science and Industry!

Thinking Ahead

Across the country, architects are cutting down on waste. They are thinking about Earth in their decisions. The architects are being very creative.

One contest-winning home design is a house that runs on spinach! The roof materials, created from spinach, collect sunlight, which powers the house.

CHAPTER 5

MATERIAL WORLD

Frank Gehry and his team of architects designed the Disney Concert Hall in Los Angeles, California. Gehry had a lot to think about. The center needed indoor and outdoor spaces. Most important was creating a concert space where sound could be heard very well.

The group worked closely with a well-known sound expert. They had to create a building in which every performance sounded its best.

Frank Gehry (left) works on a model. Behind him is a white model of his Disney Concert Hall.

The design was successful. The hall seats more than 2,000 people, but its concerts feel like close, shared experiences. It's no surprise that the project required more than 30,000 drawings!

A Sense of Place

Architects must figure out how to fit their projects into neighborhoods. They try to use materials that are available in the area. They plan for the weather. They pay attention to the setting.

Experts from different fields worked together to design the Disney Concert Hall.

Researchers are experimenting with new building materials. In the past, long, heavy beams of steel were used to provide support for a building. Now, light steel made in a frame of overlapping, crossed lines can do that and more.

Someday, designers say, your home might have a roof or walls made of "cells." Those cells could take in sunshine to produce energy.

Tools of Technology

Construction documents (CDs) are drawings that show workers how to build structures. They show the sizes of things and what goes where. In the old days, architects drew CDs by hand. They used rulers and other tools.

Now, architects create CDs with computers. **Computer-Aided Design and Drafting (CADD)** and **Building Information Modeling (BIM)** are the new

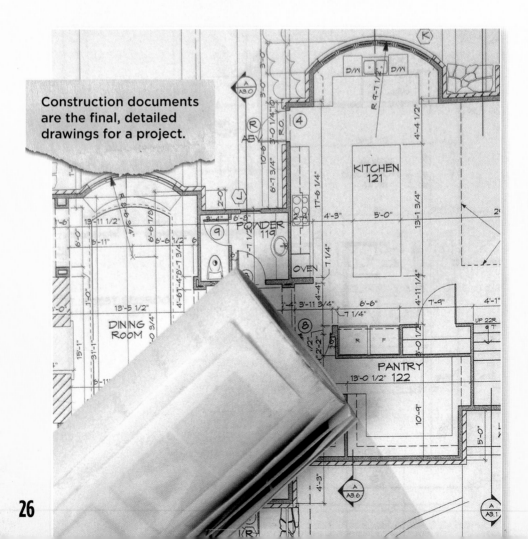

Construction documents are the final, detailed drawings for a project.

Katrina Cottages

Because of Hurricane Katrina, many people in and around New Orleans, Louisiana, lost their homes. The U.S. government moved many of those people into trailers. Some of the trailers turned out to be unsafe, so Congress paid for a project to replace them. A young architect from Alaska named Marianne Cusato came up with a winning design in 2005. The Katrina Cottage is cheaper than the trailers. It is strong. It can be built quickly. And it's better looking!

tools. CADD uses computer technology to build models with height, depth, and width. Architects also use computers to test their designs. BIM uses computers to produce and manage information about a building.

Pyramids of the Future

Have you ever looked at the ancient pyramids in Egypt? Did you wonder why we don't build those anymore? We might! In 2008, architects in Dubai, the biggest city in the United Arab Emirates, showed plans for a new pyramid. The structure would cover about 1 square mile (2.6 square kilometers). Planners say it could hold up to a million people. The structure would run on steam, wind, and other natural energy. They call this covered city Ziggurat.

Mark on the World

At the start of this book, you answered questions about your interest in this field. Here are a few more: Do you like to make plans? Do you like to work with tools of technology? Can you correct your ideas if you get new information? Do you care deeply about the future of the planet? Can you see a new world, one that is improved by architecture? Then architecture may be for you!

Do you like computers? They are an important part of the job of an architect.

ARCHITECT

OUTLOOK

- The United States had 160,000 architects in 2006. That number is expected to grow about 17 percent by 2016.

- In 2006, most architecture firms had fewer than five workers. About one in five architects worked for themselves.

WHAT YOU'LL DO

- Architects turn ideas into structures or spaces. They are responsible for a project's look, function, safety, and cost.

- Architects are the leaders of the project. They create the final construction documents (CDs). CDs outline everything from where the electricity runs to which walls have plumbing. Architects organize information and check on the building during construction.

WHAT YOU'LL NEED

- Architects need a degree from an NAAB-approved school. A five-year bachelor's degree is the most common. Some specialties, such as research, require a master's degree. If you have a bachelor's in architecture or a related field, you can add a two-year master's degree. However, if your bachelor's degree is unrelated to architecture, you need a three- or four-year master's degree.

- Architects need a license. After earning a degree, architects must practice for about three years. Then they must pass an exam for a license and follow state requirements.

WHAT YOU'LL EARN

- Architects earned between $36,250 and $112,990 in 2007. Conventional architects usually earn more than landscape architects.

Source: U.S. Department of Labor, Bureau of Labor Statistics

GLOSSARY

budget — money set aside for the cost of building a project

Building Information Modeling (BIM) — the process of producing and managing information about a building

clients — people who use the services of a professional person, such as an architect

Computer-Aided Design and Drafting (CADD) — the use of computer technology to build models with height, depth, and width

condominium — an apartment building in which the units are owned by the people living in them

construction documents (CDs) — the final, detailed drawings for a project

engineers — people who are trained to use math and technology to make useful products

green architecture — the process of designing structures that reduce the impact on people's health and on the environment

internships — periods of time when people train for work or help at a low-level job

landscape architects — people who develop outdoor spaces for human use and enjoyment

license — a permit given by law to practice something

modular — designed with parts that are made ahead of time for easy assembly and use

renewable resources — materials and energy that replace themselves, such as sunlight and the fast-growing grass called bamboo

sites — places or locations

TO FIND OUT MORE

Books

Bodden, Valerie. *Frank Gehry.* Mankato, MN: Creative Education, 2008.

Caney, Steven. *Steven Caney's Ultimate Building Book.* Philadelphia: Running Press Kids, 2006.

Fandel, Jennifer. *Frank Lloyd Wright.* Mankato, MN: Creative Education, 2005.

Manatt, Kathleen. *Architects.* Ann Arbor, MI: Cherry Lake, 2007.

Web Sites

Building Big
www.pbs.org/wgbh/buildingbig

Check out these interactive extras from PBS's award-winning show based on David Macaulay's books.

Great Buildings Collection
greatbuildings.com

Learn more about thousands of famous structures. You'll see maps, time lines, and plenty more.

Green Building
www.epa.gov/greenbuilding

Find out more about green buildings at this site run by the U.S. Environmental Protection Agency.

INDEX

About the Author

Jessica Cohn lives in Westchester County, New York, where she runs a publishing firm. The work allows her to research interesting topics and ponder new ideas, which is one of her favorite things in life. She has written books about many kinds of jobs, from aerospace workers to vocational teachers. Every job is interesting, she says, when you look at it closely!